THE
Archive Photographs
SERIES

AVRO

A.V. Roe poses with the Roe I biplane outside his shed which was Britain's first aircraft hangar. In the background can be seen the Brooklands motor racing track with the spectator seating and stands.

THE
Archive Photographs
SERIES

AVRO

Compiled by
Harry Holmes

CHALFORD

First published 1996
Copyright © Harry Holmes, 1996

The Chalford Publishing Company
St Mary's Mill, Chalford,
Stroud, Gloucestershire, GL6 8NX

ISBN 0 7524 0653 1

Typesetting and origination by
The Chalford Publishing Company
Printed in Great Britain by
Redwood Books, Trowbridge

Front cover illustration
Work under way on an Avro 501 at the Clifton Street works in April 1913.
The young man in the cockpit area is F.J.V. Holmes, great-uncle of the author.

Contents

Introduction

One of Britain's earliest aviation pioneers was Alliott Verdon Roe, born in Patricroft, Manchester in 1877. After engineering training and service in the merchant navy his interest in aviation began to grow and he had the burning desire to be the first Englishman to fly a powered aeroplane.

In September 1906 the *Daily Mail* advertised a competition for model aeroplanes capable of powered flight with the prize money amounting to £250. Roe entered the competition, held at Alexandra Palace in April 1907, winning the £75 First Prize.

On 8 June 1908 Roe confounded his critics by making a powered flight of some seventy-five feet from the motor-racing track at Brooklands in Surrey in his Roe 1 biplane.

Encouraged by his success he designed his Roe 1 Triplane and made a flight of over 900 feet on 23 July 1909. With this machine, powered by a 9 hp motor cycle engine, he became the first to fly a British aeroplane powered by a British engine from British soil.

During his early flights Roe had used Brooklands, Lea Marshes and Wembley Park, but a shortage of money forced him to return to the north. He then formed a partnership with his brother Humphrey who owned Everards, manufacturers of elastic webbing, based at Brownsfield Mill, Ancoats, Manchester.

On 1 January 1910 the brothers registered the world's first aeroplane manufacturing company, A.V. Roe & Company, and Avro, as it became known, took over the basement of Brownsfield Mill.

The brothers also rented a large shed at Brooklands for test flying of Avro types and for use as a flying school. Orders for aeroplanes did not appear as expected so the brothers established 'The Aviator's Storehouse' which supplied everything for flying machines and the requirements of would-be aviators began to materialise.

The years 1911-12 saw great achievements for Avro with the company becoming firmly established in the aviation world. The company built the Avro Type F, which was the world's first totally enclosed cockpit aeroplane. The Type D was the first British aircraft to fly off water while it was an Avro aeroplane which raised the duration record to seven hours and thirty-one minutes. In 1912 the British War Office ordered three military biplanes which meant overtime for Avro workers who produced the first machine in just eight weeks, two weeks ahead of schedule.

As interest in aviation began to grow Avro needed to expand and with financial support coming from the Groves Brewery of Salford, A.V. Roe & Company Limited was registered on 1 January 1913.

Avro moved into new premises in Clifton Street, Miles Platting, Manchester, but the outbreak of World War One in August 1914 saw the need for military aeroplanes and it soon became obvious that even the new works would be inadequate. The company then approached engineers Mather & Platt for use of their newly completed 15,000 square feet extension.

It was at this time that Roy (later Sir Roy) Dobson joined the company and struck up a friendship with a young draughtsman named Roy Chadwick. In later years the two would be synonymous with the name of Avro.

On 8 October 1914 the first aerial bombardment of Germany took place when a flight of Avro 504s raided Cologne. Towards the end of the same month the War Office placed a rush order for four Avro 504s. These aircraft were required for a secret operation and had to be fitted with newly designed bomb racks. The machines were built to specifications, crated up and left the factory for an unknown destination. On 21 November 1914, exactly twenty-three days after

Leyton Council, concerned about their image, evicted the young pioneer from the Lea Marsh site after he was classed as a crank! The move to Wembly Park proved to be a great success with longer flights able to be achieved.

the order was placed, news came through that three of the 504s had successfully raided the large Zeppelin sheds at Friedrichshafen. Such was the faith in the Avro aircraft that their first flight was made on the actual attack.

However, the 504 was destined to make an even bigger impact in the role of a training aircraft. Early in 1917 Colonel Smith-Barry of the Royal Flying Corps, concerned about the poor standard of pilots arriving on the Western Front, evolved an entirely new method of training flying instructors at the Special School of Flying at Gosport in Hampshire. This method was based solely on the use of the Avro 504 and the type became the standard trainer for the RFC and later, the RAF, until well into the 1930s.

Avro production was not confined to the 504 as the company developed other types including fighters and heavy bombers. Because of this Avro considered that the expansion taking place in Manchester was not sufficient and a new factory and airfield at Hamble near Southampton were built.

Production figures during World War One were startling and in the last year before the Armistice over 5,000 Avro machines were built. During the war period 8,340 Avro 504s were produced.

In November 1918 the victory brought fresh problems for Avro as a new factory at Newton Heath, Manchester, which was intended to produce up to 500 machines a month, was almost complete, but the cessation of hostilities meant an end to aircraft orders.

Newton Heath did open in November 1919, but because of the struggle to win what few aircraft contracts there were, the factory was employed in the manufacture of a variety of children's toys, bassinets and even billiard tables. Another venture was the building of car bodies to fit various chassis, but this work ceased when Crossley Motors Limited took a shareholding in Avro in order to eliminate this competition.

In the years immediately following the war Avro became pioneers of the 'Five Bob Flip', employing ex-RAF pilots to fly surplus 504s converted to carry two passengers. These flights were extremely popular and did a great deal to foster airmindedness throughout the nation.

The Cierva Autogiro Company of Spain was formed in the mid-1920s with their first two autogiros using Avro 504 fuselages. Avro took great interest in this type of aircraft and built a number of autogiros under licence from Cierva.

Alliott Verdon Roe sold his interest in the company in 1928 passing control to Mr J.D. Siddeley of Armstrong-Whitworth Aircraft Limited. Roe then acquired controlling interest in the flying boat company of S.E. Saunders Limited which then became Saunders-Roe.

The founder of the company was knighted in the 1929 New Year's Honours. His full name was Edwin Alliott Verdon Roe, but in April 1933, as a tribute to his mother, her maiden name was incorporated into the family name of Roe. Thereafter the family name became hyphenated into Verdon-Roe. Sir Alliott died on 4 January 1958.

In May 1918 Avro had established a flying field at Alexandra Park in Manchester on land owned by Lord Egerton of Tatton, but in 1923 the owner gave the company notice to quit as it was wanted for housing. The move had to be completed by mid-1924 and a new landing ground was urgently sought, ideally not too far from the Newton Heath factory.

A site was found at New Hall Farm near Bramhall in Cheshire and this contained a number of useful buildings plus a large field. The land was purchased and a new large building was erected for the assembly of aircraft with hangars being transferred from Alexandra Park. Avro then invited the Lancashire Aero Club to share the site. The airfield became known as Woodford.

Among the well-known aviators of the 1920s was Avro pilot Bert Hinkler who made a number of record breaking flights including the first solo to Australia flying an Avro Avian. Other personalities who flew Avro machines during their careers were Amy Johnson, Jim Mollison and Sir Charles Kingsford Smith, The Avro contribution to the growing interest in aviation was considerable as between the wars thirty-five different aircraft types were produced, excluding developments of basic types such as the Avro 504.

The floor space at the Newton Heath factory was increased by over 250,000 square feet in 1934 and by that year a succession of fine aircraft were coming off the production lines including the Avian and Cadet for club and private owners, the tutor which replaced the 504 as standard trainer for the RAF and Avro 626s for overseas military operators.

The Avro 652, a twin-engined monoplane, designed for Imperial Airways made its first flight from Woodford on 7 January 1935. At that time the Air Ministry was looking for an aeroplane to fill the coastal reconnaissance role and the 652 ideally matched the specification. Chief designer Roy Chadwick made a number of military modifications and the aircraft became the Avro 652A later given the name Anson. One of the safest machines ever built, the Anson had a production run of almost 11,000 in seventeen years of manufacture, flying in many different roles to earn the well-deserved name 'Faithful Annie'.

In 1936 Avro took up the challenge of designing a twin-engined medium bomber to the specifications laid down by the Air Ministry and this was to become known as the Avro 679 Manchester.

As the war clouds began to gather once again Avro had built a new factory at Chadderton near Oldham and in March 1939 the employees from Newton Heath began moving into the new premises. Like the previous facility, Chadderton was to manufacture the main aircraft components with wings, fuselage and tail then being transported to Woodford by road for final assembly, test flying and delivery.

It seemed strange that the first aircraft jigs set up in the new plant were not for Avro aircraft, but the Bristol Blenheim light bomber. In May 1938 Avro had been awarded a contract to build 250 of that type followed by another to produce a further 750.

The prototype Avro Manchester made its first flight from Avro's new experimental facility at Ringway (now Manchester International) Airport on 25 July 1939 and impressed the Air Ministry with its performance and advanced features.

On 3 September as Britain declared war on Germany the peace-time standards had to be abandoned as the factories quickly settled down to the serious business of mass production for the RAF.

Avro had received an order for 200 Manchesters and the aircraft in service proved to be a splendid flying machine – when the engines were working! The Rolls-Royce Vulture was plagued with problems and was one of that company's few failures. However, from this setback came the greatest bomber of World War Two, the Avro Lancaster. When Rolls-Royce cancelled development of the Vulture, Roy Chadwick looked to the Merlin engine, which was successfully powering the Spitfire and Hurricane, to equip this excellent airframe. Both powerful and reliable, the Merlin was smaller than the Vulture and it would require four for the new bomber which originally was known as the Manchester III. By the time of its maiden flight in 9 January 1941 the name Lancaster had been adopted and the flight trials proved to be a complete success. The four Merlins were perfect giving the aircraft an excellent performance which so impressed the Air Ministry that the Lancaster was ordered into mass production.

The only actual raid on an Avro factory was at Chadderton on Easter Monday 1941 when the *Luftwaffe*, in the shape of a lone Junkers 88, found its target. The bombs hit the stores area, but no one was injured as the workers had that day for holiday instead of the previous Good Friday. Surprisingly, the vital assembly plant at Woodford was never bombed although its location was known to the Germans as aerial photographs of the airfield were taken in October 1940. The Metropolitan-Vickers plant at Trafford Park was attacked disrupting production of the Avro Manchester for a short period.

As transport aircraft were required for the RAF, Avro used Lancaster-type wings and tail fitted to a newly-designed fuselage suitable for carrying loads as the basis for the Avro York. This aircraft first flew from Ringway on 5 July 1942 and proved itself to be a reliable aeroplane which was later used by Churchill, Lord Mountbatten, Field Marshall Smuts and other war leaders. After the war it did sterling service during the Berlin Air Lift.

In 1944 the labour force involved in building Avro aircraft was over 40,000 with Lancaster production averaging 150 per month. Anson production continued with manufacturing being transferred to Yeadon (now Leeds/Bradford) Airport with that type's deliveries peaking at 135 per month. By the war's end Lancaster production, including 430 built in Canada, totalled 7,377. Lancasters took part in all of the famous raids of World War Two and also dropped two-thirds of the total tonnage of bombs dropped by the Royal Air Force from 1942 to 1945.

Japanese expansion in the Far East brought new problems for the Allies and it was decided to develop a super Lancaster which would fly faster, farther and with a greater bomb load. This aircraft, the Avro Lincoln, made its first flight on 9 July 1944, but was too late to see action in the war. The aircraft did serve with the RAF and the Royal Australian Air Force until the mid-1960s.

As the war ended it soon became apparent that the British were behind the field in air transport. The first British 'airliner' was the Avro Lancastrian, a stop-gap version of the Lancaster, which went into service with Trans-Canada Airlines, later, with BOAC, Qantas and British South America Airways.

The first custom-designed airliner from Avro was the Tudor, but this aircraft was greatly restricted by directives from the government that the aeroplane had to use as many Lincoln components as possible. The original customer, BOAC, cancelled their order as the Tudor did not fill their requirements and Roy Chadwick made numerous changes to improve the design making the airliner more economical to operate and with larger capacity. Tragically it was in one of these developments, the Tudor II, that he met his death in a take-off crash at Woodford on 23 August 1947. His death left a great gap in British aviation and his passing was felt by all in the industry.

Although the Tudor was classed as a failure, it was later versions of the aircraft, together with Avro Yorks, which led Britain's contribution during the Berlin Air Lift after the Russians had blockaded the city leaving the air as the only access for food and supplies. The Tudor vindicated itself during that period.

Immediately after the war the one field in which Britain reigned supreme was in the design and production of the gas turbine or jet engine. For a decade after the war practically all new engines were tested on Avro aircraft and, in later years, an Avro Vulcan was used as a flying test-bed for the development of the Olympus engine used by Concorde.

One of Chadwick's last designs was the Avro 696 Shackleton which took to the air for the first time on 9 March 1949 under the command of chief test pilot Jimmy Orrell. He could never have imagined what a magnificent servant this aeroplane would be as the type would serve the RAF for over forty years with the last four only being retired in 1991.

On New Year's Day 1947 the RAF issued a specification for a four-jet bomber. In a bold step, Roy Chadwick produced a design for a delta-winged aircraft which would become known as the Avro 698 and despite its unusual shape it met all of the design requirements. After his death, the design team now under Stuart Davies set about refining the aircraft's shape into the configuration so familiar in later years as the mighty Vulcan.

The Vulcan had its maiden flight on 30 August 1952 in the capable hands of Roly Falk. It is now history that the Vulcan went on to be the backbone of RAF Strike Command providing Britain's nuclear deterrent for over two decades. It was only used once in anger and this came in the twilight of its career with an attack on Port Stanley during the Falkland's war in 1982. This raid entered the record books as the longest combat mission ever undertaken with the lone Vulcan making a round trip of 8,000 miles and all in complete radio silence. It is a record never likely to be beaten!

The Defence White Paper of 1957 stated that there would be no more manned bombers for the RAF, so Avro decided to look at the civil market once more. A review of the air transport industry showed a requirement for an aircraft which could replace the famous Dakota. The new aircraft would have to operate from unpaved runways and go anywhere a Dakota could, but with twice the payload and with higher safety standards. The answer came with the Avro 748, a regional airliner capable of carrying up to sixty passengers or six tons of freight. Powered by two Roll-Royce Dart turboprops the aircraft was extremely economical and reliable to operate. The 748 first flew on 24 June 1960 piloted by Jimmy Harrison and has since lived up to all expectations. With safety and reliability its greatest features it is not surprising that the 748 was chosen as the transport for no fewer than sixteen Heads of State. The ubiquitous 748 continued in production until 1988 with nearly 400 sold to 50 countries around the world. The 748 was the last aircraft to bear the name Avro and even today is known in some parts of South America as 'El Avro'. A military rear loading version of the 748 was built and served with RAF and RNZAF as the Andover C.1. A specialised version is known as the Andover E.3.

In 1963 it was decided to rationalise most of the main aircraft manufacturers into two companies, Hawker Siddeley Aviation and British Aircraft Corporation with famous names like Avro, Blackburn, de Havilland, Folland, Gloster and Hawker being absorbed into the former. Thus Avro became Hawker Siddeley Aviation, Manchester, overnight! In 1977 the two large companies were themselves amalgamated becoming British Aerospace and proud of their history the two ex-Avro factories at Chadderton and Woodford continue as part of that great organisation.

One
The Beginning

Alliott Verdon Roe's career in aviation started when he won the major prize of £75 in the *Daily Mail* Model Competition held at Alexandra Palace in April 1907.

After initially planning on a 6 h.p. power plant for his biplane, A.V. Roe fitted this 9 h.p. motor cycle engine. This did not provide enough power to lift the aircraft and the machine was eventually fitted with a borrowed 24 h.p. Antoniette.

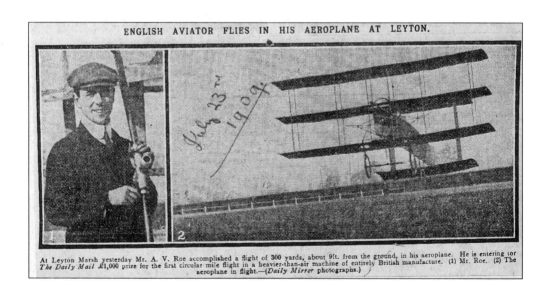

ENGLISH AVIATOR FLIES IN HIS AEROPLANE AT LEYTON.

At Leyton Marsh yesterday Mr. A. V. Roe accomplished a flight of 300 yards, about 9ft. from the ground, in his aeroplane. He is entering for *The Daily Mail* £1,000 prize for the first circular mile flight in a heavier-than-air machine of entirely British manufacture. (1) Mr. Roe. (2) The aeroplane in flight.—*(Daily Mirror* photographs.)

The newspaper photographs tell the story of Roe's most successful flight of the period – he would have flown further, but some rapidly approaching trees forced him to land as he had not yet learned how to turn his aeroplane!

Roe and his helpers prepare the Roe I Triplane for flight at Blackpool in October 1909. The Bullseye title on the machine was the trade name for the men's braces manufacturer owned by his brother Humphrey.

The young aviator surveys his wrecked triplane after one of his frequent crashes. The accident happened at Wembley Park in December 1909.

Roe poses with his 35 h.p. Green engined Roe III in September 1910. Harvard University of the USA ordered one of this type, but this had to be rebuilt after Roe crashed it soon after delivery.

The single seater Avro Type D at Brooklands before the Circuit of Britain air race in July 1911. Unfortunately, the aircraft crashed before the race as hastily fitted wing extensions to the lower wing became detached during a test flight.

This Type D seaplane owned by Commander Oliver Schwann, RN, at Barrow-in-Furness in August 1911. After a number of failures the aircraft became the first seaplane ever to take off from British seawater.

Test pilot Fred Raynham seated in the fourth Type D at Brooklands in October 1911. Standing by the machine is Sydney Sippé who became famous by taking part in the first bombing raid of World War One while flying an Avro 504.

Not an usual sight in the early days of aviation! An Avro Type D came to grief at Brooklands in 1911. The banked racing track can be seen in the distance.

A Type E is transported from Brownsfield Mill through Manchester's cobbled streets to London Road (now Piccadilly) station for the train journey to Brooklands in February 1912.

Early in 1912 it was decided to change to company's type numbering system with the first aircraft to benefit from this change being the Avro 500. Asked why it started at 500, A.V. Roe replied, 'It was drawing office swank!' The photograph shows an Avro 500 flying at the Central Flying School, Upavon in 1912.

Lt. Wilfred Parke, RN, in the cockpit of an Avro 500 at Old Trafford 1912. The demonstration was given to allow Avro workers to see one of their machines in flight.

Another view of the Avro 500 at Old Trafford, Manchester. Interested onlookers surround the aircraft which was flying from a field outside the works of Robert Carlyle Ltd..

An aeroplane which used the earlier type designation was the Avro Type G biplane. There had been no chance for a test flight before the aeroplane was delivered to Larkhill to take part in the Military Aeroplane Competition in August 1912. The Type G won the erection time test, but failed in the climb performance trials. The company, however, was awarded £100 for taking part in all the tests with an untried machine!

Avro also built aeroplanes of other people's designs and this Curtiss-type biplane was known as the Lakes Waterhen. It was built in 1911 for Capt. E.W. Wakefield and operated from Lake Windermere.

A single-seat Type E, known as the Avro 500, and this aircraft was delivered to No. 3 Squadron at Netheravon in April 1913. No.288 was the second in a five aircraft contract from the War Office.

As the company's fortunes improved through new investment and orders, Avro moved into new premises at Clifton Street, Miles Platting, Manchester in March 1913. The staff photograph was taken when the move was complete and includes both Alliott and Humphrey Verdon Roe to the left of the young lady in centre front while Roy Chadwick and Reg Parrott are on the right of her.

The original Avro 503 seaplane moored at Shoreham in June 1913. The aircraft interested the German Navy with a licence agreement allowing Gotha to build the type as the WD.1, which was used against the Allies during World War One.

Two

The Avro 504

The first of many! The prototype Avro 504 in September 1913 showing the original square-shaped engine cowling and warping ailerons.

An historic photograph showing the three Avro 504s at Belfort, France before their attack on the Zeppelin Sheds at Friedrichshafen in November 1914. The aircraft were completed by Avro, shipped out and the raid carried out in less than twenty-three days, in fact, the actual operation was the first time the machines had ever flown!

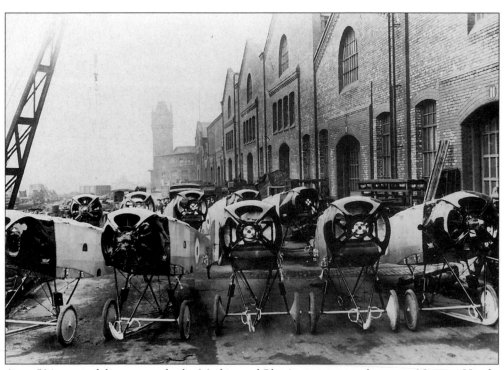

Avro 504s await delivery outside the Mather and Platt's engineering factory at Newton Heath, Manchester. This works was used by Avro when extra floor space was required.

The Avro 504 was mass produced after the type had been selected as the standard trainer for the Royal Flying Corps. A shortage of engines forced Avro to look at a universal mounting for power plants with the same airframe becoming an Avro 504J or K version.

A fine study of an Avro 504 in flight. This aircraft was rebuilt by Avro for the film *Reach for the Sky* which told the life story of Sir Douglas Bader. The aircraft still flies regularly as part of the Shuttleworth Trust.

The Avro 504 was the principle aircraft of the élite flying school established at Gosport to teach instructors the art of training their pupils to a higher standard.

A brand new Avro 504K photographed just after it had emerged from Avro's new facility at Hamble near Southampton.

After World War One ended many Avro 504s were sold to civilian owners for passenger carrying and pleasure flying. Avro ran its own small airline for two years and many of the public made their first flight in this type.

The first aerial inspection of a sheep herd in Australia took place in September 1920 when a prospective customer hired an Avro 504K to check the stock before buying!

Australia's national airline QANTAS commenced operations with this Avro 504 which was powered by a Sunbeam Dyak engine in place of one of the radial types.

A post-war development was the Avro 504L training seaplane which was basically a 504K mounted on floats, but with increased fin area to improve handling.

Although the Air Ministry showed no interest in the Avro 504L, the aeroplane did equip a number of civil operators and was used for passenger and joyriding flights in Southern England and the Lake District. This photograph was taken at Hamble in September 1919.

The Type 504M was yet another modification, this time with covered accommodation for the pilot and two passengers. Despite the enclosed advantage, the cabin was cramped and only one aircraft was converted by Avro. One was also converted in Japan and was used for several years.

A much improved version of the 504 was the Avro 504N which became the standard basic training aircraft for the Royal Air Force until the 1930s. This machine, built by Parnall & Son of Bristol as an Avro 504K, was modified to the new model.

This aircraft was the first of the Armstrong Siddeley Lynx-powered interim prototypes for the Avro 504N. Modified from a 504K, the machine still retained its skid undercarriage.

Export orders for the Avro 504N exceeded expectations with contracts from around the world. Here, four aircraft for the Royal Hellenic Navy Air Service await delivery from Woodford in June 1925.

Air Shows grew in popularity during the 1920s and here Flight Lieutenant John Fogerty shows the 'crazy flying' routine at Hendon in July 1927.

A fine example of an Avro 504N can still be seen in the Arsenal Museum at Copenhagen. The aircraft was delivered to the Danish Navy in 1927 and, miraculously surviving German occupation, is on display alongside other early aircraft.

An unfortunate pupil's first solo ended like this! The Avro was from No.4 Flying Training School which is still active today flying BAe Hawks from Valley, Anglesey. A few civil Avro 504Ns were impressed into the RAF in 1940 and did valuable work on early radar calibration trials.

The prototype Avro 504O, not surprisingly, was the float-plane version of the 504N. Pictured on its first flight from Hamble in 1924, this type was supplied to Chile, Japan and Greece.

In July 1924 a specially designed seaplane designated the Avro 504Q was delivered to Spitzbergen in the Arctic Circle for use by the Oxford University Expedition of that year.

The final model of the type was the Avro 504R which was a lower powered version for civil operations. Known as the Gosport, the aircraft first flew in June 1926 and became popular with a number of flying clubs.

Though the Gosport was initially designed for civil operators, it was sold to the military of Estonia, Peru and Argentina with the latter producing a further 100 in a licence-build arrangement. The aircraft in the photograph was flown by Lancashire Aero Club from Woodford, but was involved in a fatal crash in October 1928 after the passenger had tried to take over the controls.

This trio of large twin-engined aircraft was shot at Hamble in March 1917 and are, left to right: the Avro 523 Pike, with the pusher propellers; an Avro 523A with tractor airscrews; and the Avro 529. The war was ending as these types reached the end of their test programmes and no production was forthcoming.

Chief designer Roy Chadwick, a pilot himself, loved to fly and especially in an aeroplane of his own design! He is seen here on the right of the picture with Hamble general manager Reg Parrott (centre) and test pilot Fred Raynham ready to fly the Avro 529A.

Designed as a two-seater reconnaissance aircraft for the Royal Flying Corps, the Avro 530 first flew at Hamble in July 1917. Problems with stability required a number of modifications and the machine is seen in its final form, but was not developed further.

Also designed specifically for the RFC, the Avro 531 Spider was a lightweight fighter with an excellent performance. Unfortunately, the Sopwith Snipe had already been selected by the service and this aeroplane later emerged as a racing machine with the type number Avro 538.

The Avro 533 Manchester appeared as result of trials with both the Type 523 and 529. It first flew in December 1918, but the ending of World War One saw no requirement even though service trials had been excellent.

Three
Problems of Peace

Roy Chadwick anticipated the requirements for a light aircraft for private flying once the war was over and he proudly poses with the Avro 534 Baby. The photograph was taken shortly before its maiden flight in April 1919.

Naturally, the seaplane version of the Avro 534 was known as the 'Water Baby' with the designation Type 534A. The aircraft is seen on Southampton Water in November 1919 and performed well despite a steady increase in weight due to water soaking into the floats.

An Avro Baby fuselage and tail surfaces were used by a Mr H.G. Leigh for trials with a small mainplane and a Venetian blind-type arrangement using six narrow-chord wings. Nothing is known of the trials, but the aeroplane seems to have interested Avro test pilot Bert Hinkler shown here with Mr Leigh in December 1920.

The Avro 539 racing seaplane was designed to take part in the 1919 Schneider Trophy Race, but due to float damage it became the reserve aircraft. However, it was not to matter as the race was abandoned due to fog and the aeroplane, later fitted with a land undercarriage, became the Type 539A.

'If it looks right it flies right!' A famous axiom of the aircraft industry and what better example could there be than the Avro 547! This commercial aircraft with an enclosed cabin for four passengers was the victim of heavy financial restrictions forcing the company to use as many 504 parts as possible. The prototype was completed in February 1920, but the performance was poor and only two machines were built.

The dreadful Avro 547 had Pride of Place on the Avro stand at the Olympia Show in July 1920. Much interest was shown and the prototype was actually sold to QANTAS, much to the airline's regret! Also on the stand are an Avro Baby and a Type 548 displayed as the Avro Tourist.

The Type 548 again owed much to the Avro 504 as surplus airframes were converted into the Avro Tourist. The aircraft in the photograph won all three races at the Croydon Aerial Meeting in September 1921 and was later operated by Giro Aviation for joyriding off Southport sands until 1935.

Avro employee Miss Elsie Mackay poses for a glamour shot of the time for the company's magazine *Joystick* in 1922. The aircraft in the background is an Avro 548.

The first military aircraft to be designed by Avro after the war was the Type 549 Aldershot a large bomber powered by a single Rolls-Royce Condor engine. In 1922 flight tests on the Mark I, as shown in the photograph, revealed a lack of lateral stability and this was cured by lengthening the fuselage.

Fifteen Avro 549B Aldershot IIIs went into RAF service with No. 99 Squadron in 1924. This shot shows the prototype Aldershot after it became a Mark IV by changes in the wings and the installation of a Beardmore Typhoon engine. This machine later went to Farnborough as an engine research aircraft.

One of the Aldershot IIIs of No. 99 Squadron at Bircham Newton in 1924. The Avro type was eventually replaced in the squadron by the Handley Page Hyderabad in April 1926.

An unusual shot of the Avro 552 seaplane which, as it can be seen, relied heavily on the 504. A landplane version was known as the Type 552A, but it was the floatplane which had most success as it was ordered by the Argentine Navy and licence-built in Canada.

A special order came to Avro with the requirement for a small seaplane to take part in the Shackleton-Rowett Antarctic Expedition of 1921. As the aircraft needed strengthened floats and folding wings the solution came in the shape of the Avro 554 Antarctic Baby. Seen with this aircraft, left to right: Reg Parrott, Major James Carr (expedition pilot) and the very dapper Roy Chadwick.

A carrier-based fleet spotter was the role of the Avro 555 Bison. Twelve Mark Is were built to Air Ministry specifications in 1922 and a further forty-one Mark IIs followed in 1924-25. This Bison is flying off HMS *Argus* during fleet exercises in the North Sea during September 1924.

Originally conceived as a torpedo bomber, the Avro 557 Ava was eventually classed as a coastal patrol aircraft when changes in torpedo size made such a large aircraft unnecessary. Only two prototypes were built and this nostalgic picture shows the first machine at the RAF display, Hendon in the July 1927.

Designed by Chadwick specifically for the *Daily Mail* Light Aeroplane Trials held at Lympne in October 1923, the Avro 558 was a neat biplane. The machine flew well, but only two were ever built due to poor engine reliability and ground handling problems.

Alliott Verdon Roe himself designed his answer to the Light Aeroplane competition with the Avro 560 monoplane which could use short (thirty feet) span wings for racing or extended (thirty-six feet) wings for longer duration flights. This photograph shows Bert Hinkler preparing to fly the aeroplane.

The Roll-Royce Condor III engine newly fitted into the Avro 561 Andover, a transport version of the Aldershot. A redesigned fuselage to accommodate twelve passengers or six stretchers then used all other components of the Aldershot.

The Light Aeroplane Trials loomed again in 1924 with the Avro entry being the Type 562 Avis. The Avis was not a great success, being fitted with four different engine types during its lifetime.

Avro opened its new aerodrome at Woodford for the first time in 1925. Sharing the airfield with the Lancashire Aero Club the two were able to put on a fine display for the spectators. Landing is an Avro Gosport while a D.H. 60 Moth is in the foreground and in the distance can be seen the usual 'fort' which was always successfully bombed by the RAF at air shows.

The civilian counterpart of the Type 561 Andover was the Avro 563 which was similar to the military aeroplane, but having twelve seats in slightly more comfort. The type was evaluated by Imperial Airways, but in 1927 it was sold to the RAF to join the three Avro 561s already in service.

One of the most attractive fighter biplanes of its day was the Avro 566 Avenger. Along with two other new fighters, a Hawker Hornbill and Gloster Gorcock, the Avenger appeared at the 1926 display at Hendon. However, with budget restrictions in the RAF no new fighter was selected. This photograph shows the Avenger II in 1928.

The beautifully clean lines of the Avenger II are apparent in this photograph. This aircraft gained second prize in the 1928 King's Cup Air Race. Note the machine gun recessed into the fuselage seen after a demonstration of its fighter potential.

The Avenger's agility was ably demonstrated by Flight Lieutenant Frank Luxmore's spirited display at the Hampshire Air Pageant held at Hamble in May 1928.

Assembly of the Avro 571 Buffalo in 1926. The photographer had requested that the workers face the camera and keep perfectly still, but the emerging no nonsense Roy Dobson told him, 'Don't keep them standing around for too long!'

A private-venture design for a carrier-borne torpedo bomber, the Avro 571 Buffalo took part in military trials at Martlesham late in 1926, but once again Avro lost out as the competition was won by the Blackburn Ripon. Improvements were made to the Buffalo and after conversion to a seaplane the aircraft was bought by the Air Ministry in 1928 and was used for experimental work at Felixstowe.

It wasn't all work! Avro had, and still has, an excellent Sports and Social Club. In the mid 1920s the company had a rented field near Macclesfield for weekend use and, here, some of the employees' wives and children join Newton Heath works manager John Lord and young Roy Dobson on the old 'fun' car which provided many happy hours.

Autogiros had always interested A.V. Roe and he became great friends with its Spanish inventor Don Juan de la Cierva. After early experiments in Madrid using a basic Avro 504 fuselage and tail surface, much interest was shown by the Air Ministry resulting in Avro producing a number of types under licence. This shot shows a Cierva C.8L which was built as the Avro 575.

Alliott Verdon Roe seen at Hamble before the first flight of the Cierva C.6 (Avro 574) autogiro in June 1926.

The prototype Avro 581 Avian underwent a number of changes in shape after being designed for the Light Aeroplane Trials of 1926. The improvements brought with it numerous record flights and Bert Hinkler, seen here in the Type 581A, liked the aeroplane so much that he bought it from Avro for £750. After making some of his own modifications he made a record breaking flight to Australia in 1928. The aircraft is now preserved there.

The move to Woodford was not without its difficulties for Avro as the facility had no water or electricity available and, in fact, the latter was not supplied until 1933... nine years after the company arrived on the site! The hangar shown survives to this day as part of the flight sheds.

In 1926 the Air Ministry specification for a single-seat fleet fighter was answered by the Avro 584 Avocet, an attractive all-metal, stressed skin biplane with interchangeable wheel or float undercarriage. Performance of the Avocet was unimpressive and only two were built with the second machine, fitted with floats, used for practice by the RAF's Schneider Trophy team.

This aircraft was actually the fourth Gosport built. It was fitted with an Avro Alpha 100 h.p. engine and strengthened undercarriage to become the Avro 585. Then, to publicise flying as a safe means of transport, Bert Hinkler landed the aeroplane on the summit of Helvellyn (3,118 ft.) in December 1926. This shot shows the machine returning to Woodford after the flight.

The complete redesign of the Avro 581 warranted a change in type number with the aeroplane becoming the Avro 594 Avian. The aircraft was excellent, but the D.H. 60 Moth had over a years start on the Avian in the highly competitive club and private market. However, the Avian was an attractive machine and more than held its own on the sales front.

The Avro 594 established a number of records and this aeroplane 'John', an Avian III, was photographed at Croydon in June 1928 shortly before a delivery flight to South Africa. The pilot, Lt. Patrick Murdock, SAAF, delivered the aircraft without incident and, unknown to him, set up an England to Cape Town record taking just $13\frac{1}{2}$ days.

This aeroplane, J9182, was the only Avro Avian to be supplied to the RAF. The aircraft, a Mark IIIA was delivered in October 1927.

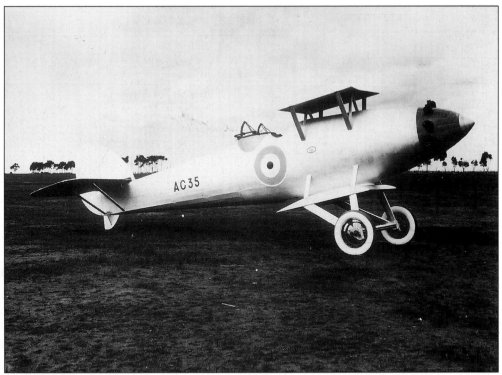

A full-scale mock-up of the projected A.C. 35 army co-operation aircraft which was to be built in Australia to the Avro 590 design. It was a promising project, but was not built as the British Military Commission insisted that any Australian requirement must be met by aircraft built in Britain.

Another mock-up, this time of the Avro 604 Antelope, was built at Hamble to meet a specification for a high-performance two-seater day bomber for the RAF.

The Antelope made its first flight in November 1928 and, although it performed well in the competition, it lost out to the Hawker Hart. The aircraft was allocated to the Royal Aircraft Establishment and provided valuable data testing various engines.

The Prince of Wales, later King Edward VIII, visiting the factory at Hamble in 1929. The autogiro in the foreground was a Cierva C.19 Mk.II which, although built by Avro, did not receive a type number.

The seaplane version of the Avian III was given the type number Avro 605 and, here, the prototype is taking off from Southampton Water after its launching at Hamble in 1928.

The Avro 616 Avian IVM designed for overseas markets had a strengthened structure with tubular steel replacing wood in the basic airframe. The aircraft sold well on the export market and was assembled both in Canada and the USA.

After visiting Fokker in Amsterdam, Avro management was impressed by the design and welded steel tube construction of the Fokker VII trimotor. The company acquired the licence to build it for sale in the British Empire with the designation Type 618 or Avro Ten, as it was popularly known in relation to the number of seats. This aircraft was photographed in April 1931.

The Avro factory at Newton Heath, Manchester with production in full swing during 1931.

A scaled-down version of the Avro 618 was designed by Roy Chadwick and, not surprisingly, it was known as the Avro Five. The Type 619 had accommodation for a pilot and four passengers.

The woodworker's apron was still the main attire in the 1930s with an Avro Five wing being built at Newton Heath.

Wilson Airways of Kenya operated this Avro Five named 'Knight of the Grail' on local services from Nairobi. A modified version was the Type 624 or Avro Six.

Another view of the shop floor at Newton Heath showing the basic airframe for Avro 621 Tutors while in the rear are two fuselages for Avro Fives.

Tutors, Avians and Avro Tens are all in the course of manufacture at Newton Heath in 1932. In the previous decade business had been slow, but there seems little available space in this shot.

After the great success of the Avro 504, Roy Chadwick designed another excellent training aircraft in the Avro Tutor. The aircraft became the standard trainer for the RAF and an early customer was the Irish Air Corps who renamed it Triton for their service use. The photograph shows the second prototype.

A seaplane version of the Tutor was tested at Hamble and also at the Marine Aircraft Experimental Establishment at Felixstowe. Tests were highly successful and resulted in an order from the Air Ministry for fourteen machines which were designated Avro 646 Sea Tutors.

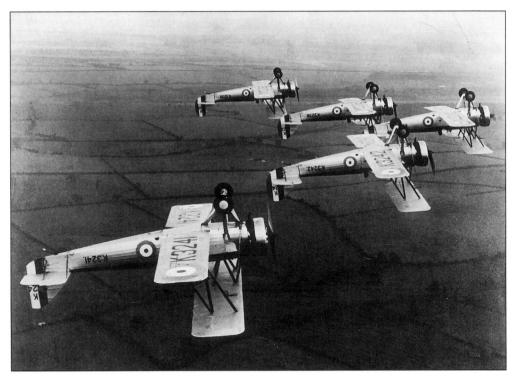

Tutors flown by instructors of the Central Flying School at Upavon during some inverted formation flying. The team's aerobatic routine was excellent with the Tutor's delightful handling qualities making it a worthy successor to the Avro 504.

From the Avian IVM came a modified version known as the Sports Avian and a number of this type competed in air races including the 1930 King's Cup. Another modification was this Avian monoplane which was built specifically for air racing and was designated the Avro 625.

The Avro Tutor formed the basis of an aircraft which was to be capable of meeting the requirements of smaller air forces. The Avro 626 was a general purpose machine ideal for some of the military operators which required a maid-of-all-work type of aeroplane and export orders kept the Avro production lines busy.

The Avro 626 was a multi-role aircraft aimed at the military market, but there were a few exceptions as ex-demonstrators were quickly sold after becoming surplus to the company. This machine was flown by the Earl of Amherst and based at Heston.

The Avro Prefect was navigational training version of the Type 626 and this photograph shows the first of the seven ordered by the Air Ministry. Four others were supplied to the Royal New Zealand Air Force and one still flies regularly at air displays in that country.

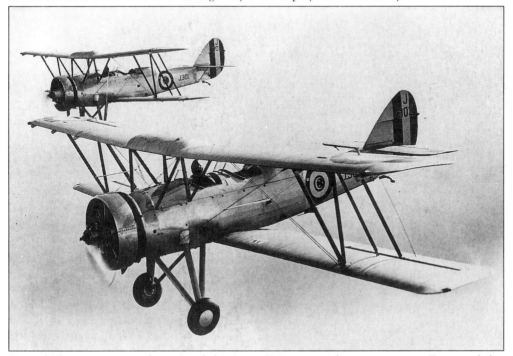

One of fifteen countries who ordered the Avro 626, or one of its variants, was Egypt and this shot shows the first two of thirty-one ordered for that country on a test flight from Woodford in October 1933.

The Type 627 Mailplane was designed for the use by Canadian Airways, but after contractual difficulties, the order was cancelled. The aircraft was later re-designed as the Avro 654.

Roy (later Sir Roy) Dobson, a tough Yorkshireman, was the backbone of A.V. Roe & Company Limited after the departure of Alliott himself in 1929. His much deserved Knighthood came in 1945 for his contribution to the war effort. This portrait shows him in 1934.

Another type which owed much to the Tutor was the Avro 631 Cadet which was designed for private or club flying and was available from 1932. An improved version introduced in 1934 was the Avro 643 Cadet II and an excellent order came from the Royal Australia Air Force for thirty-four of that type.

The six Avro Cadets supplied to the Irish Air Corps in 1932 are seen lined-up for review at Baldonnel.

Air Service Training at Hamble was the largest civilian user of the Cadet with sixteen of this type used for basic flying training, blind flying and aerobatics.

Another type aimed at the smaller air forces was the Avro 636. Designed by Roy Chadwick as a dual purpose aircraft, four of this type were delivered to the Irish in 1935.

Avro test pilot Sam Brown makes a low fast run over Woodford in the first Avro 636. This type was operated by the Irish until at least 1941 serving alongside their Gloster Gladiators.

This interesting shot shows the Avro 626 demonstrator G-ABJG wearing the trials (Class-B) registration K-10. The aircraft was being used as a development aircraft for the Type 637 hence the armament and bombs.

An Avro 638 bought by the Airwork School of Flying is seen on its delivery flight from Woodford to Heston in June 1933. The three aircraft in the order were flown in formation for the delivery.

A close-up of the dual control cockpits of an Avro 638 Club Cadet of the Midland & Scottish Air Ferries Limited.

A variation of the Club Cadet design was the Avro 639 Cabin Cadet which had an enclosed cabin for the pilot and two passengers. This aircraft was never certificated and was later rebuilt as a standard Club Cadet.

The Type 640 was a three-seat version of the Cadet with side-by-side seating for passengers in the front cockpit. The aircraft was seen at Woodford before delivery to the Scottish Motor Traction Company Limited in April 1933.

Many people were made aviation-minded by the famous National Aviation Day displays staged by Sir Alan Cobham's 'Flying Circus' and the photograph shows one of his two Avro 640s.

This beautiful little cabin biplane is the prototype Avro 641 Commodore which first appeared in May 1934. A total of six were built with two seeing war service as communications aircraft with the RAF.

The Commodore's cabin layout was unusual in having two pilot seats, but only one control column which could be swung from side to side. Two passengers could be carried, or three if less baggage went along.

An evocative shot of the busy Newton Heath production line in May 1934 shows an Avro 671 (Cierva C.30A) autogiro, a floatplane version of the Avro 626 followed by two Commodores.

The Type 642 airliner was known initially as the Avro Eighteen, indicating the number of seats – two pilots and sixteen passengers. Only one twin-engined version was built and delivered to Midland & Scottish Air Ferries in 1934. It was later sold in the Far East and provided excellent service before it was destroyed by the Japanese in New Guinea during 1942.

A four-engined Avro 642 was sold to the Viceroy of India, Lord Willingdon, in December 1934. Named 'Star of India' the aircraft was impressed in RAF service in September 1939, but was withdrawn one year later after it was found that the wing was being eaten away by ants!

Imperial Airways issued a specification to Avro for a small, fast, mail carrying airliner with a retractable undercarriage. The first of two Avro 652s was delivered to the airline in March 1935, but it could never have been imagined that this type would be the forerunner of one of the most famous Avro types – the Anson.

The first production Anson Mk.I at Woodford after test pilot Geoffrey Tyson had taken the aircraft on its maiden flight on New Years Eve 1935.

Another view of the first production Anson which would be followed by almost 11,000 more in over seventeen years of manufacture.

The Avro 652 for Imperial Airways became a bonus for Avro as the design almost matched the Air Ministry specification for a coastal reconnaissance aircraft. Chadwick suitably modified the drawings with a few minor changes and the addition of a mid-upper gun turret and the Avro 652A Anson was born. The first Ansons in service were with No. 48 Squadron at Manston, Kent in 1936.

An aerial view of the Newton Heath factory which was custom-built during the production expansion of World War One. It was company headquarters from 1919 until the massive new facility was opened at Chadderton in 1939.

Work underway on Ansons and Blenheims at Newton Heath in the late 1930s. As the war clouds were looming aircraft factories became busier than ever.

The licence-built Cierva C. 30A was the Avro 671. One of the first customers was the Air Ministry who initially ordered ten, later increased to twelve. Known as the Avro Rota in the RAF the aircraft did valuable work during World War Two helping to calibrate every coastal radar station from Orkney to the Isle of Wight.

Always willing to take on work, Roy Dobson secured a contract to build 287 Hawker Audax army co-operation biplanes. Chadwick later designed the aircraft to take the Armstrong Siddeley Panther radial engine in place of the Roll-Royce Kestrel and twenty-four of this type were supplied to the Egyptian Army Air Force as the Avro 674.

The airfield at Woodford seen early in 1939 with Ansons, Blenheims and a Cadet on the ground. The hangars in the photograph are today part of the flight sheds complex.

Avro chief test pilot Sam Brown awaits completion of the final engine runs before taking the first Avro-built Bristol Blenheim into the air for its maiden flight in September 1938. The trilby-hatted gentleman was Woodford works manager Arthur Ainsworth.

Workers are holding down the tail of the Blenheim Mk.I as the engines are run at full bore. Avro built 250 of this version then went on to produce a further 750 Blenheim Mk.IVs.

Deputy chief test pilot Bill Thorn during an inter-factory flight in an Anson. He was to be promoted when Sam Brown retired in 1945.

Four
The War Clouds Gather

King George VI tours the Blenheim production line at Newton Heath in March 1939. His Majesty is accompanied by Roy Dobson and Sir Frank Spriggs, chairman of the Hawker Siddeley Group. Three rows behind are Roy Chadwick and Teddy Fielding, the small gentleman in spectacles, who masterminded Lancaster production throughout the war.

The busy scene at Woodford as Ansons and Blenheims are lined-up awaiting test flights or delivery.

An Avro Anson as many wartime aircrew would remember it, although this one is slightly different as it is the prototype Mark IV which had been fitted with American Wright Whirlwind engines in place of the normal AS Cheetahs.

Awaiting the first flight of the Avro 679 Manchester bomber in July 1939 are three of the key players in the aircraft's development, left to right: Charlie Hatton (production manager), Sandy Jack (chief inspector) and Stuart Davies (assistant chief designer).

Designed to an Air Ministry specification, the Avro Manchester stands ready for its first flight at Ringway in July 1939. Although it was an excellent flying machine, the aircraft was plagued by engine problems throughout its life as its powerplant, the Vulture, was one of Rolls-Royce's few failures.

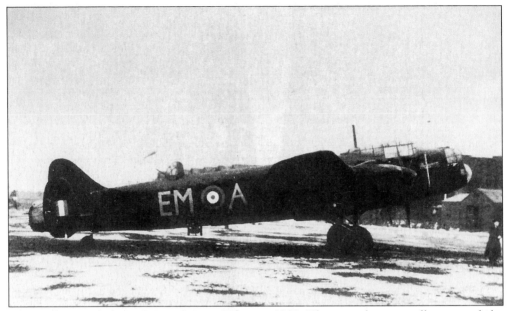

A Manchester of No. 207 Squadron in February 1942. This aeroplane actually survived the engine problems to become something of a record with thirty-three operations completed – the most for the type. However, the failure of the Manchester was instrumental in the birth of a Legend – the Avro Lancaster.

These airmen have a lot of work ahead of them repairing the flak damage on this Manchester of No. 61 Squadron. The aircraft had been involved in an attack on German battleships in February 1942.

One of the many versions of the Anson was the Mark XI which had a deeper fuselage with increased headroom. This aircraft was completed as an air ambulance with a hinged wing root door to allow stretcher cases to be loaded into the cabin.

Chief test pilot Sam Brown about to remove the rotor arm from his car as a precaution. This interesting photograph shows Woodford's flight sheds' ramp under construction while on the field are two Manchesters, a Havoc and an Anson.

A rare shot of a Douglas Boston operated by Avro. This aircraft was engaged in fuel jettison trials which were undertaken by the company after securing the contract to convert Douglas DB-7s from a Belgian order into Havocs and Bostons for the RAF.

The prototype Avro 683 Lancaster in its original triple-finned form at Boscombe Down in January 1941. Just one month later the aircraft was flying with the twin fins which became the standard configuration. The aircraft in the background is a Blackburn Roc.

The magnificent Lancaster was
undoubtedly the finest bomber of
World War Two. Many of its raids
are legendary and Lancasters
dropped two-thirds of all bombs
dropped by Bomber Command from
1942 to 1945.

In November 1942 King George VI
and Queen Elizabeth visited the
Lancaster production lines at
Woodford. Her Majesty is seen
chatting to Roy Chadwick under the
nose of his most famous creation.

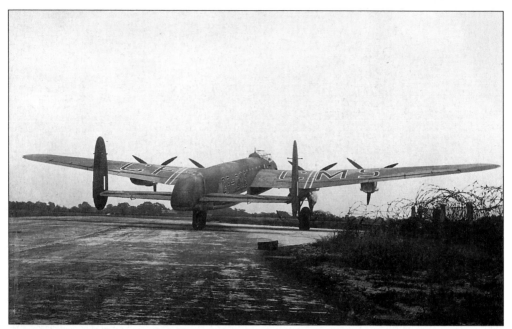

A Lancaster was flown to Canada to act as a pattern for production of the bomber in that country. It was later converted for civilian use as a mail carrier becoming the forerunner of the Avro Lancastrian, a stop-gap airliner version of the famous bomber.

A popular visitor to Avro was Mrs Eleanor Roosevelt, wife of the President of the United States, who spent much of her time talking to the workers at Chadderton and Woodford. She even asked Woodford's canteen manageress for the recipe of her apple pie!

Avro's own Anson, used as a communications aircraft, was lovingly known within the company as 'Aggie-Paggie' referring to the aeroplane's registration letters. This aircraft was the first Mark 19.

The requirement for wartime transports aircraft prompted the design of the Avro 685 York and this photograph shows the prototype nearing completion in Chadderton's experimental department.

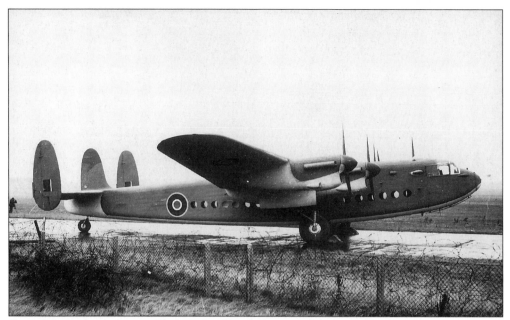

One of the early production Yorks behind barbed-wire at Ringway. The use of Lancaster wings and tail are evident in this shot with the central fin being added to improve handling after changes in flying characteristics by the introduction of the large slab sided fuselage.

The Minister of Aircraft Production, Sir Stafford Cripps, visited the Avro factories in the Manchester area and then on to Ringway to view the York. Sir Stafford is seen talking to Roy Dobson and J.B. Caley, Avro's contracts manager.

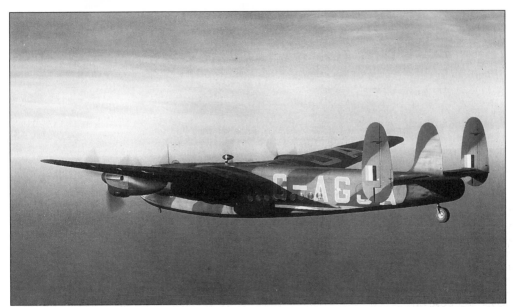

The first York to go onto the civil register retained its military camouflage while serving with BOAC. This version was a passenger/freighter with accommodation for twelve passengers in the rear of the cabin, the first civil flight being made from London to Cairo in April 1944.

Yorks did sterling service after the war, the photograph showing an aircraft of Skyways operating charter flights for BOAC. This type is also remembered for its great work in the Berlin Air Lift.

Originally named Lancaster IV, the Avro 694 Lincoln made its first flight from Ringway in June 1944 in the very capable hands of Sam Brown. The aircraft was designed for operations against the Japanese in the Pacific, but the war ended before the aeroplane could be used in anger.

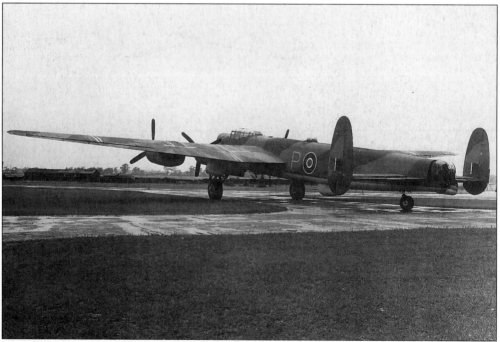

Another view of the prototype Lincoln which clearly shows the increase in dimensions over its predecessor. With the Lancaster production in full swing the change-over to the Lincoln was slower than expected with the corresponding entry into the RAF service.

Although the Lincoln was too late to see action in World War Two, the aircraft did serve with the Royal Air Force until the mid 1960s. The aircraft shown was operated by the Bomber Command Bombing School in 1959.

'Aries II' the Lincoln serving with the Empire Air Navigation School at Shawbury was unusual as it was fitted with Lancastrian nose and tail fairings. It was in this role that the aircraft established a number of long distance records.

A number of Lincolns were used for experimental purposes with this aircraft engaged in development work on the probe and drogue air-to-air refuelling system. The photograph shows the aircraft refuelling an F-84 Thunderjet of the USAF.

As the war drew to its close Lancasters were converted into stop-gap airliners with the name Lancastrian. Chadwick designed a simple modification designated Avro 691.

The first Lancastrian at Woodford shortly before delivery to BOAC at Croydon in February 1945. Its cabin accommodation was for just thirteen passengers which today would be the capacity of a small commuter aircraft.

BOAC acquired the Lancastrians for the long distance routes, mainly Australia, and here the first aircraft is loaded with mail before departing for Sydney. The airline operated seventeen Lancastrians before they were eventually replaced by custom-designed airliners.

As with the other Avro heavies, the Lancastrian was used for the development of gas turbine engines. Rolls-Royce converted two for trials with the Nene engine in the outer nacelles in a similar arrangement to this aircraft which was flown by the de Havilland Engine Company to test their new Ghost engine.

During the Berlin Air Lift Lancastrians were converted to liquid carriers each capable of transporting 2,500 gallons of petrol or diesel. The experts in this field were Flight Refuelling Limited who supervised the whole fuel operation.

he Avro 688 Tudor 1 was conceived in 1943 as an interim airliner for the North Atlantic route with the maiden flight in June 1945. Pictured here, the prototype completes its final engine runs at Ringway on the morning of the flight.

A close-up of the installation of the Roll-Royce Merlin 102s on the prototype Tudor 1 which was Britain's first pressurised airliner.

The sleek Tudor 1 awaits clearance to start engines for the aircraft's first flight which, surprisingly, was made without any registration markings.

Congratulations for Bill Thorn from the Tudor's designer Roy Chadwick after the maiden flight. Following Thorn out of the aircraft are Jimmy Orrell and flight engineer Arthur Bowers. Chadwick and Thorn were to die together in the crash of another Tudor just two years later.

Elizabeth of England was one of the Tudor 1s ordered by BOAC, but the airliner did not meet their requirements and the order was cancelled in April 1947. The Corporation demanded more and more modifications and the normally placid Chadwick was furious as many could have been incorporated initially if there had been more consultation.

After problems with directional stability Chadwick increased the tail surface area and this can be seen here in this shot of a Tudor 4 of British South American Airways. The fin was not as pretty, but was much more efficient!

A line-up of Avro machines at Ringway in 1945 are, left to right: Lincoln, Lancaster, Tudor 1, Lancastrian, York and Anson.

A higher capacity version, with a stretched fuselage, was Avro 689 Tudor 2 designed for the Empire routes. First flight was in March 1946 with the aircraft having the original tail configuration similar to the Mark 1. Similar problems forced the change as on the earlier aircraft.

The team involved in the Tudor 2's maiden flight were, left to right: Alf Stewart (experimental manager), Bill Thorn (chief test pilot), Roy Chadwick (chief designer), Teddy Fielding (production director), Jimmy Orrell (deputy C.T.P.), Arthur Bowers (flight engineer) and Jack Dobson (production manager).

The tragic crash of the Tudor 2 at Woodford in August 1947 robbed the aviation industry of some of its greatest talent. Besides the loss of Roy Chadwick, the company also lost chief test pilot Bill Thorn, co-pilot David Wilson and radio operator John Webster. Happily, Chadwick's deputy Stuart Davies and engineer Eddie Talbot, survived. Crossed ailerons during maintenance caused the disaster and this great loss was felt all over in aviation.

In order to improve the performance of the Tudor 2 the Merlin engines were replaced by Bristol Hercules radials and in this shot Jimmy Orrell brings the Tudor 7 in for a fast, low run over Woodford. The Avro Tudor vindicated itself in the freighter role during the Berlin Air Lift.

Post-war Chadderton, the headquarters of Avro, proudly displays the company name. Built as the war clouds gathered, the factory did not show its name for obvious reasons, but of course, the *Luftwaffe* certainly knew where it was located!

As the war ended Coastal Command required a long-range aircraft for maritime reconnaissance after return of the Lend-Lease Liberators to the United States. Avro's answer was the Type 696 which became the Shackleton. Here, the prototype flown by Jimmy Orrell, makes a low pass over Woodford on return from its maiden flight in March 1949.

The first Shackletons on the production line at Woodford in March 1950. In the background are four Lancasters in for refurbishment and at the far end is a Tudor.

Brothers in Arms! On the brow of Woodford's famous sloping ramp is a production Shackleton MR.1 and a Lincoln B.2 photographed in May 1951.

A production Shackleton MR.1 flies low over the Mersey estuary in June 1951. The area was excellent for test flights as the search radar could be tested on the many vessels using the Port of Liverpool.

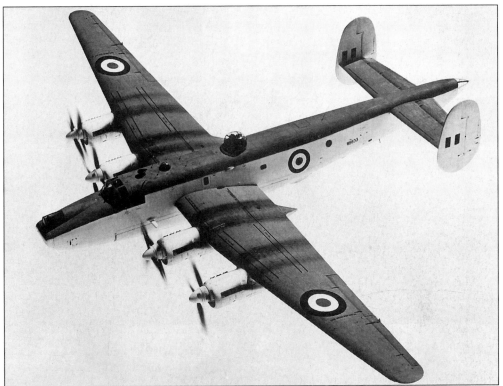

The Shackleton MR.2 was a redesign of the earlier version which had a number of improvements including a reshaped nose, which could be fitted with twin cannons and the repositioning of the ASV search radar to the aft of the weapons bay. The first production MR.2 flew in June 1952.

An exciting time at Woodford as preparations are made for the departure of a Shackleton MR.2 and Vulcan to take part in the 1953 Farnborough Air Show. The Shackleton is equipped with an airborne lifeboat and test pilot Johnny Baker amazed spectators at the Show by flying the aircraft on one engine. More about the Vulcan later!

The Shackleton MR.3 was a departure from earlier models as it had a tricycle undercarriage and wing-tip fuel tanks to give longer endurance. This type was outlived by the MR.2 as the extra fatigue caused by the tip tanks forced them into retirement earlier than expected.

Avro had excellent overhaul and repair facilities at Bracebridge Heath, Lincolnshire and Langar, Nottinghamshire, and it is at the latter that this photograph was taken in June 1958. It shows just how extensive overhauls were as these Shackletons have been completely stripped down.

In March 1989, the five remaining Shackletons returned to Woodford to celebrate the type's fortieth anniversary. These aircraft were the AEW.2s which was the designation of the airborne early warning version and this shot shows one of the aircraft, with the author on board, leaving Woodford to return to its base at Lossiemouth, Scotland. It could never have been imagined that Shackleton would be in RAF front-line service until they were retired in 1991.

An RAF requirement to replace the Harvard as the standard advanced trainer was met by Stuart Davies with the design of the Avro 701 Athena. The aircraft used the turboprop Mamba or Dart engines in its Mark 1 form while the Athena 2 had a Merlin piston engine. This production Mark 2 was evaluated by the RAF's Central Flying Establishment in October 1949.

Both versions of the Athena are lined-up outside the Woodford Club House during a visit by senior RAF officers in 1949. Although twenty-two of this type were built, the large RAF order went to the Boulton Paul Balliol.

Still going strong in 1952, this Avro Lancaster of No. 683 Squadron is seen over Mount Kenya. The Squadron did much valuable work photographing and mapping a number of areas in Africa.

The Avro Tudor did achieve fame when, in September 1948, the type became Britain's first four-jet transport aircraft. The second prototype Tudor 1, which had been converted to the longer Mark 4, was later fitted with four R-R Nene jet engines to emerge as the Tudor 8. Jimmy Orrell displayed the aircraft at the 1948 SBAC Show at Farnborough just a few days after its first flight.

Before his death, besides designing the Shackleton, Roy Chadwick made the initial design for the four-jet delta-winged bomber known as the Avro 698. The handling characteristics of a delta were largely unknown at that time and Avro resolved to build a small research aircraft of one-third scale of the new bomber. This type, the Avro 707, made its debut at Farnborough in September 1949.

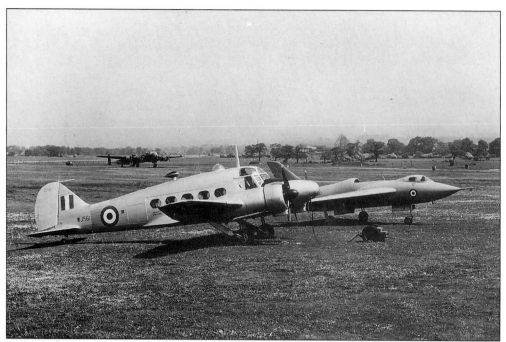

A peaceful scene at Woodford in May 1952 which shows the last Anson shortly before delivery, an Avro 707B and, in the distance, an Avro Lincoln.

In all there were five Avro 707s built including, the first prototype, two 707As for high-speed research, a 707B for low-speed work and this aircraft, the Avro 707C which was a two-seat side-by-side aeroplane for delta familiarisation flying. All provided valuable research for the Vulcan programme.

Six uncompleted Tudors provided the basis of the four-jet Avro 706 Ashton programme. The six aircraft, all in different roles, contributed a wealth of aeronautic knowledge during their various experimental tasks. The type first flew in September 1950.

Jimmy Orrell, one of the greats of test flying, with the prototype Ashton some time after the maiden flight. During a career spanning over thirty years he flew more than a 100 different types of aircraft and from 1942 to 1945 he personally tested more than 900 different Lancasters!

Five

The Mighty Vulcan

A big day for Woodford as the Avro 698 is rolled out for the first time. Stuart Davies designed the aeroplane as we know it and the tall gentleman in shirt-sleeves is Roly Falk who would be the first to fly it in September 1952.

The prototype Avro 698, now named Vulcan, roars in for a landing at Woodford after an early test flight. The new shape in the skies caused a certain amount of consternation in many parts of the country as numerous sightings of a UFO were reported to the police!

The Vulcan prototype with four Avro 707s in a formation routine for the 1953 Farnborough Air Show. The straight leading edge on the bomber's wing was later cranked to provide greater wing area.

The first production Vulcan awaits its crew on a balmy day at Woodford in July 1955. Some of the flight test engineers enjoy the moment until take-off arrives.

Extending the range of the Vulcan was an early improvement and here a Vulcan B.1 takes on fuel from a Vickers Valiant tanker during trials in June 1959.

A massive fire at the Chadderton factory in October 1959 destroyed many offices including the central records which held all the company's historical documents and the photographic department which lost over 47,000 negatives. Although the main factory roof came down, amazingly, Vulcan production was only slightly delayed.

The Avro Blue Steel stand-off missile was also produced for the RAF's V-Bomber force and is here fitted to the underside of a Vulcan B.2 of the famous No.617 (Dam Busters) Squadron.

Conscious of disturbing local residents with the Vulcan's mighty roar during engine runs, Avro installed this muffling unit which deflected the jet blast upwards reducing the noise level.

The RAF's last Vulcan paid its final visit to Woodford just before it was retired from flying in 1993. Despite a concerted effort to keep the aircraft flying for display purposes, the mighty machine was eventually grounded as part of government economy cuts. Happily, it is lovingly cared for at Bruntingthorpe, Leicestershire, in the hope that one day it will again grace the skies.

It was a sad day in October 1956 when the last Lancaster was retired from RAF service and, after a ceremony at St Eval, Cornwall, it was flown to Wroughton to be scrapped.

The sleek Avro 720 mixed jet and rocket powered interceptor fighter in Chadderton's experimental department in 1956. The aircraft was in an advanced stage of completion when further development was cancelled in government cuts.

Another project which was a victim of the economy cuts was the Avro 739 low level strike aircraft which is seen here in model form during wind-tunnel tests at Woodford.

Designed as a replacement for the Vickers Viscount airliner, the Avro 771 would have been a sixty-passenger aircraft powered by two Bristol Siddeley BS.75 jet engines. Further development ceased as Avro concentrated its resources on the Avro 748.

As previously noted, Sir Roy Dobson was never one to refuse any work for Avro and from 1953 for the following two years the company built seventy-five Canberra B.2s under licence from the English Electric Company Limited.

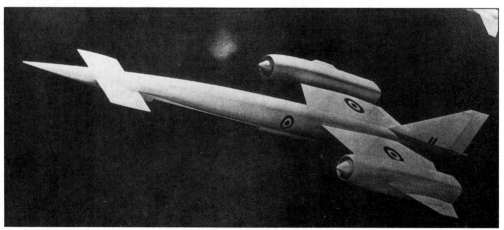

The economy cuts hit hard throughout the British aviation industry, but none more than at Avro. The futuristic Avro 730 supersonic bomber would have been powered by eight jets. The illustrated Avro 731 would have been a three-eighths scale development aircraft for the 730 and the former did reach the test rig stage before both were cancelled in 1957.

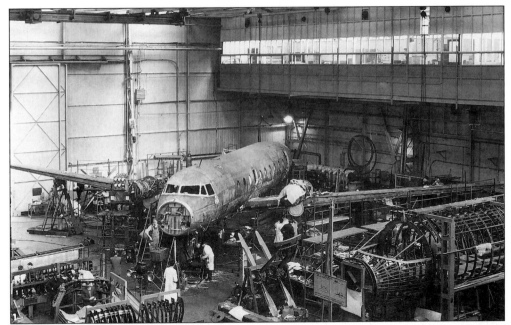

One private-ventured project which went on to great success was the Avro 748 twin-turboprop airliner. The aircraft was designed as a result of the 1957 Defence White Paper which stated that there would be no more manned bombers for the RAF and Avro began to look at the civil market once more. The company's studies revealed a need for a modern aircraft to replace the Douglas DC-3 series and the Type 748 emerged. In this photograph the prototype nestles in one corner of Chadderton's experimental department in January 1960.

The Avro 748 made its first flight from Woodford in June 1960 with chief test pilot Jimmy Harrison at the controls. The flight was made just seventeen months after the go-ahead for the project and the aircraft had a fine start as the maiden flight lasted two hours and forty-one minutes, which was a record duration for the initial flight of a civil airliner.

The world's most reliable turboprop engine, the Rolls-Royce Dart, powered the Avro 748 and as orders were achieved the Woodford production lines were busy again after Vulcan and Shackleton assembly had ended. Eventually almost 400 were sold in fifty countries throughout the world.

The first military customer for the Avro 748 was the Brazilian Air Force who ordered six in 1962 with a re-order for a similar number in later years. In 1992 they celebrated thirty years of accident-free flying with the 748 and could see no need to replace this reliable workhorse.

Another early customer for the Avro 748 was BKS Air Transport Limited which operated from Leeds/Bradford Airport. The company was on the verge of collapse when the arrival of the first 748s produced a turn-around of the airline's fortunes. BKS eventually expanded before being taken over by another airline which was then itself absorbed into British Airways.

The reputation for safety and reliability of the 748 was widely acknowledged as the aircraft was used by no less than sixteen Heads of State including Her Majesty the Queen. The three Queen's Flight 748s were known as Andover CC.2s.

A licence-build agreement with India was for the 748 to be assembled by Hindustan Aeronautics in Kanpur with production reaching eighty-nine aircraft for the Indian Air Force and Indian Airlines. This photograph shows the first locally built Series 2 for the airline.

Although the Lancaster was retired from the RAF service, enthusiasts in Britain were still treated to the occasional sight of a visitor from the Royal Canadian Air Force. This aircraft called in at Waddington in 1962.

Woodford is an excellent site with over 450 acres, large assembly shops, flight sheds and a 7,500 ft. main runway. The New Assembly, as it is known, is over one million sqaure feet in area and boasted three production lines, each one a quarter of a mile long. Still in use by British Aerospace for Regional Jet manufacture, the name of Avro has been revived for this unit.

A military development for the ubiquitous 748 was the rear-loading Andover C.1. Originally designated Avro 748MF, it was given the number Type 780 after significant changes in the aircraft which included a 'kneeling undercarriage' for ease of loading up the rear ramp. The type is operated by both the RAF and the Royal New Zealand Air Force.

The massive factory at Chadderton near Oldham also has over a million square feet of assembly shops and offices. The plant is still very active as Chadderton Aerostructures, a division of British Aerospace.

No story of Avro would be complete with the mention of Avro Canada which was formed when the company purchased Victory Aircraft Limited as production of the Lancaster ended in 1945. The new company went on to produce some fine aircraft including the advanced Avro C-105 Arrow, shown here. However, in 1959, a change of government saw the programme cancelled forcing Avro Canada into closure thus depriving the country of an irreplaceable part of its aircraft industry.

The driving force behind Avro, Sir Roy Dobson, retired in 1967 at the age of seventy-five! His energy and vitality were well-known throughout the aviation industry and his Knighthood, received in 1945, was thoroughly deserved.

Three Avro legends seen together for the last time before the Shackleton and Vulcan were retired from flying. It is of great satisfaction to many that the Lancaster continues to fly as part of the RAF's Battle of Britain Memorial Flight as a tribute to the brave men who flew them and, of course, to those who built them. The aircraft should please air show crowds for many years to come after its complete overhaul in 1996. It is interesting to note that the aircraft's wings were reconditioned at the Lancaster's place of birth, Chadderton. Where else!

AERIAL DERBY MEETING.

THE

AVRO BABY

:: WON ::

FIRST PRIZE - - - - - - - - 1919
FIRST and SECOND PRIZES - - - - 1920
in *THE ROYAL AERO CLUB HANDICAP.*

THE AVRO BABY

which flew in both the above races was the identical machine which flew from

LONDON TO TURIN in $9\frac{1}{2}$ Hours

(650 miles on 20 Gallons Petrol).

A. V. ROE & Co., LIMITED.

London Office—	AVRO WORKS,	Experimental Works—
166, PICCADILLY, W. 1.	Newton Heath, Manchester.	HAMBLE, SOUTHAMPTON.
Telephone: - Regent 1900.	Telephone: - City 8530.	Telephone: - Hamble 18.
Telegrams: - "Senalpirt, 'Phone."	Telegrams: "Triplane, Manchester."	Telegrams: - "Roe, Hamble."

Australian Agents—Australian Aircraft & Engineering Co., Ltd., Union House, 247, George St., Sydney, N.S.W.
Telephone: City 2572.   Cable Cipher: "*Aviation, Sydney.*"